Unless otherwise note
Version of the Bible.

Printed in The United States of America. All rights reserved under the International Copyright Law. No part of this book may be reproduced or transmitted in any form or by any means, electronic, mechanical, including photocopying, recording, or by any information storage and retrieval system without the written permission of the publisher.

For Publishing or Consulting contact us at:
LadiApostle Ministries, LLC
LAM Consulting & Publishing
9350 Bay Plaza Blvd., Ste. 120
Tampa, FL 33619
813-444-3751
Email: TheLadiapostle@gmail.com

©**2015 Tami Robinson, LadiApostle Ministries, LLC**
LAM Consulting & Publishing
9350 Bay Plaza Blvd., Ste. 120
Tampa, FL 33619
USA

*Dedicated to my Daughters; Shanucey, Angel & Taelor
And my lil' ladies (granddaughters) Mar'Shauny & Aubreii*

Always know that you are anointed to give birth! It's a Ladi's Legacy! I love you all more than life itself.

Table of Contents

Dedication   3
Introduction   5

1. Fruitful, Yet Barren   9

2. Finding Purpose Beyond Misery; *The Reuben Syndrome*   16

3. Hated by Man, Loved by God   27

4. A Cry For Intimacy   39

5. Purposed Birth Praise…This Time   55

6. The Importance of the Judah Assignment   72

7. Avoiding Emotional Pitfalls & Setbacks   85

Judah's Prayer   103

Introduction

Since the beginning of time giving birth was a sign that women were blessed by the hand of God. This was a woman's single most important purpose in life; her ability to give birth, reproduce and replenish the earth. The ability to give birth was also identified by the painful lives of women who were barren. Throughout scripture many women suffered through the effects of intimidation, inferiority, frustration and depression due to their inability to give birth.

Sarai before her name was changed to Sarah was one of the first women to be known as being barren according to scripture. Sarah was barren most of her adult life, and then Abram (Abraham), her husband, received a word from the Lord that she would birth their promised child. Nevertheless, Sarah was faithless and looked unto Hagar to give birth to the promise. Although Sarah chose Hagar, God had already chosen

Sarah! So many like Sarah have been given a sure word to birth promise yet they can't conceive the vision due to their impaired faith. They do not believe that God will do what He has promised. In the instance of Sarah's experience, in which she gives birth after her child bearing years, others who were barren in the bible are proven to serve a faithful God. He fulfills promise after promise and vision after vision for those whom it seems as if there was no physical possibility of being able to reproduce.

    Contrary to those who were physically barren, this book looks at the life of Leah who is apparently on the opposite end of spectrum. Leah was very fruitful physically nevertheless she was barren spiritually. Some would say that she may have been too fruitful, seen by her inevitable need to give birth to child after child. Yet in her mind she was barren, void of her desired fulfillment. She became wife by way of deceit and tradition. The eldest and not so pretty daughter of Laban had to compete with her beautiful sister whom her husband Jacob loved and desired. So, Leah ends up competing for Jacob's affection the only way she knows how.

As we take an in depth look at the life of Leah, we began to see an entirely different perspective of a woman with a God given ability and strength that was hidden by the spirit of intimidation, inferiority and rejection. Leah was given a gift by God because He saw her pain and in return gives her a miracle; He opened her womb. *And when the Lord saw Leah was hated he opened her womb..., Gen. 29:31).*

This was a natural ability that Leah was given, nonetheless we have the spiritual ability to give birth to visions, dreams, and purpose beyond our natural comprehension if we tap into our God given abilities.

I pray that as you read you find your portion that will impregnate a new seed of promise in your spirit. It is your calling to give birth to visions and purpose that please God.

Read and listen to the Holy Spirit carefully as you discover essence in the life of Leah and her true purpose as a woman forsaken by man that caught God's attention in her oppressed and uncomfortable position.

As Leah's life is explored please see the true crux of her spiritual beauty. In this discover you will tap into your inner spiritual beauty and the gifts of God will began to unfold as He reveals to you what's needed through the revelation of Leah's true gift and call.

You are not insignificant, abandoned or forgotten. God desires your purpose to be fulfilled in the earth as a testament of His power and glory. Prayerfully you will discover on a deeper level, what God truly desires for your life.

Chapter One

Fruitful, Yet Barren

Genesis 29:31- And When the Lord saw that Leah was hated, He opened her womb but Rachel was barren.

The story of Jacob is well known by many. The story encompasses the life of Isaac's son and his apparent deception in receiving a birthright meant for his eldest brother. However, as Jacob began to walk into adulthood, he is given a dose of his own medicine as he is deceived into marrying the eldest daughter of Laban, his mother's brother.

Jacob leaves his father's house with the stolen blessing from Isaac and the birthright of Esau. Isaac sends Jacob away and orders him to find a wife from the household of his mother's father (Gen. 28: 1-7). As Jacob reaches his destination he comes to a well where there are men watering their flocks, he inquires about his uncle Laban and is pointed in the direction of Laban's daughter who is approaching the well to water the sheep. Jacob sees Rachel and is immediately overwhelmed by her beauty. He greets Rachel with a kiss, and then she unites him with her father Laban. Laban greets Jacob with open arms and ask him if there is anything that he can do for him for his service. Jacob asks for Rachel as his wife and agrees to serve Laban seven years for Rachel's hand in marriage. Incidentally, it sounds like a beautiful love story in the making, although things do not go as planned.

    The recollection of this story tells that Jacob serves Laban seven years, but they seem as only a few days because of his love for Rachel (Gen. 29:20). Jacob then requests his wife, Rachel from her father Laban. Laban throws a big party and feast for Jacob and supposedly Rachel's wedding celebration. In the evening Laban takes his daughter Leah and her maid Zilpah to Jacob, who unknowingly consummates with Leah. In the morning Jacob awakes and discovers that he has just consummated his marriage to Leah and not Rachel. A confused and bewildered man he was to make this discovery.

When Laban is confronted by Jacob, Laban explains that by tradition the eldest daughter must marry first, and this was his reason for giving Leah and not Rachel. Laban then required that Jacob complete one week with Leah, and for an agreement to serve another seven years he would in turn give Rachel to him. Of course, Jacob agrees to his request and is granted the wife of his choice Rachel.

Could you imagine being Leah? The issue wasn't the fact that Jacob or Leah had no say so in choosing their mate because during this dispensation the majority of all marriages were arranged. However, Leah's situation was a more complicated one. She was given out of tradition and apparent deceit to a man who had his heart set on marrying her younger more beautiful and desirable sister.

Leah already knows that she is not working with all the right stuff. Perhaps she doesn't have the coke bottle shape, or maybe she doesn't have the long flowing hair or right toned skin. We are not sure of her other imperfections, but we do know that she was born with a deficiency that would follow her for the duration of her life, *Leah, the girl with the lazy eye*. For the rest of her life, she would be reminded her of her imperfection and of course, her sister's beauty. *Genesis 29:17- Leah was tender eyed; but Rachel was beautiful and well favored.*

How much attention did Jacob really pay to his new undesirable wife Leah? It doesn't take a genius to figure out that Jacob was most likely resentful and angered by Laban's betrayal and manipulation. Leah was a daily reminder of his disdain for his father in law and the fact that the woman he had set his heart on having for seven years, was not the one he received. Now he has agreed to serve this manipulating father-in-law for another seven years! The plans were altered and Leah was the one who would seemingly suffer most.

God in His infinite power and greatness take all of this

into consideration and He does something noteworthy for Leah. ***Gen. 29:31- And when the Lord saw that Leah was hated, He opened her womb: but Rachel was barren.***

God saw all that Leah would have to endure and He decides that although she may not be the prettiest, and she definitely may not be the people's choice, but one thing she will be is fruitful. She wouldn't be barren. Leah, although she knew she wasn't all that, knew that being able to give birth was what every woman in her day identified as a badge of honor. She had an ability Rachel did not have. Rachel was barren and the ability to give birth would be Leah's secret weapon. Leah began to use the weapon of reproduction and fruitfulness to gain the attention of her husband.

Even with this most empowering advantage Leah still felt inadequate. This same epidemic is evident in the lives of many today. Although, God has given great abilities and talents, the rejection from those who are superior in their eyes frustrates their God given purpose. If the purpose of God can be seen past personal inadequacies and physical flaws, lives of many will be used beyond their physical ability.

The gift to give life is a most precious gift given only by God and it must not be abused or misused. As God has given most women the physical organs to carry a baby and nurture it in their wombs, God then empowers them to give birth, cultivate, love and protect these babies. Coincidentally, God also gives His people the spiritual gift of reproduction.

A woman's directive given from the beginning is to be fruitful and multiply. Since we, as God's people, are considered as His bride, we are to give birth to ideas, visions and ultimately His plan and purpose. Birthing God's will is a Kingdom mandate. The enemy's mission is to cause miscarriages, still born births, abortions, and most of all, deformed visions, dreams and purpose. If he cannot kill, steal or destroy the baby (vision and purpose), he desires to cause neglect, abuse and misuse of this great gift. Leah almost neglects the purpose of her divine empowerment by using the gift of fruitfulness to accomplish the fulfillment of her emotional desire; gaining the affection, attention and connection of her uncaring husband. She gave birth to one baby after another intending to win the affection of Jacob. Leah didn't realize that every single delivery of every baby was a vision ordained by God, birthed into the world to complete a supernatural assignment.

God never sees us as man sees us. He finds the beauty of whom and what we are well beneath the surface of our flesh. God saw Leah's opposition. Anytime God views His children as wounded, He steps in and gives us power beyond our natural ability. God takes what man may despise and uses it to His advantage to further the kingdom and to give Him glory. Leah is an example of God's compassion expressed because of man's disdain of her.

Chapter Two

Purpose beyond Misery; the Reuben Syndrome

Gen. 29:32- So Leah became pregnant and gave birth to a son. She named him Reuben, for she said, "The Lord has noticed my misery, and now my husband will love me. (NIV)"

The bible states that "the Lord opened" Leah's womb. There are believer's that don't realize the anointing of purpose on their lives when they are faced with physical and social challenges. All they can see are the challenges, road blocks and obstacles that are forever before them. They sometimes neglect to challenge their trials with the word and purpose that has been invested in them.

God empowers Leah for a purpose. Leah, because of her own low self-esteem, distorts this purpose in an attempt to meet her emotional need. Purpose has many definitions. To name a few; purpose can mean the reason for which something exists or is done, made, or used. Purpose is also defined as a desired result; end; aim; or goal. The definition that illuminated the essence of Leah was the definition; *use or function of an object.*

Comparing Leah to an object may seem belittling. To Jacob she may have been seen as an obstacle and an object. Nonetheless, if we look at how she fit into the whole spectrum of Jacob's life, she was an object or an obstacle used to get to his desire, Rachel. Rachel was Jacob's place of total fulfillment and Leah presented herself as an object and an obstacle that interfered with his total and complete happiness with Rachel.

Gen. 29:25- When morning came, there was Leah! So Jacob said to Laban, "What is this you have done to me? I served you for Rachel, didn't I? Why have you deceived me?"

Gen. 29:26- Laban replied, "It is not our custom here to give the younger daughter in marriage before the older one.

Jacob's commitment to Leah was that of an obligation to tradition and more because he had to fulfill an obligation due to deceit that would render him the desire of his heart.

Many may be able to identify with Leah, as she enters this pseudo-covenant relationship with a man who is only dedicated to her out trickery and tradition. There are those who walk around and no one will ever know how defeated they are spiritually. No one will never know that as spiritual as some people may present themselves, they still feel like objects for the church, objects or obstacles in their marriages; insignificantly used day after day, month after month only to complete one project, assignment or duty after another without any true value. Just like a tool, a screwdriver, or a hammer is instrumental in constructing a foundation, but irrelevant once the job is done, it is usually thrown back into the toolbox until there is another project. Just as Leah, some have been assigned a specific use or function and they immediately fall into the trap of feeling that their lives are only defined by the needs and agendas of others.

Your purpose is not defined by any persons' need or

desire for you. Don't be blinded by their inability to see the full potential of God's purpose in your life because you define your essence through the eyes of others.

Jacob may have only seen Leah as a hindrance. The enemy gave Jacob the illusion that Leah was preventing him from receiving his true desire. Therefore, as he interacted with his wife of tradition, he did as much as was required of him in order to get Rachel.

The illusion of spiritual insignificance in a Believer's life is their greatest enemy. The enemy wants you to feel unimportant. When I made a decision to serve Christ to the fullest, the enemy made it a point to magnify my weaknesses. I saw myself as being too unworthy and too sinful. My mistakes were known by everyone, so therefore I wasn't good enough to be used by God. All that I was trying to leave behind was ever before me. Although I realized that I was pregnant with purpose, the enemy worked overtime to keep the cloud of misery from my past in my view. So regardless of how much I loved God, and how much I desired to wholeheartedly serve Him there were constant reminders of why I would never be good enough for Him. Just as Leah was hated and God saw the disdain the enemy had for her and opened her womb, God sees our disregard and He has done the same for us.

Reuben came forth as the first born son of Jacob and Leah. He was the heir of the inheritance birthed by the wife of deception. ***Gen. 29:31- And Leah conceived and bare a son named Reuben, for she said, "The Lord has noticed my misery, and now my husband will love me."*** Leah realizes that the Lord has seen her circumstances. In spite of this, she had yet to understand to the full degree, that she was anointed to birth purpose. Why is this so hard? It is increasingly difficult because we have been plagued by the traditions and opinions of man. Leah was hindered by tradition. Leah was used because of tradition and most of all used as an object of deceit. The eldest daughter must be the first to marry! Leah is caught in an unsavory love triangle. Her entire essence as a woman and a wife was mocked. Then having to compete with her younger more beautiful and desirable sister, Leah fights back with a vengeance to be the one her husband will find need of.

Okay, let's be imaginative and see what Leah could have been thinking; *"I'm not pretty, I'm not even the one that he desired. He hates that fact that he has to serve my father for another 7 years and he possibly looks at me as being the culprit. After all, if I hadn't been the eldest he could have gone on with his plans to marry Rachel and live happily ever after. I will never be what he wants, but Rachel can't give him what I can! I'm the first wife and I can give him children, she can't. So, I will have his baby and then he will see that I'm the one he should love and cherish."*

This is just a look into the minds of so many who have felt neglected and rejected by the ones' they love. Leah uses her gift to give birth as a way to win Jacob's approval. I call this ***The Reuben Syndrome;*** using a God given ability to birth a child to win the approval of man is seen throughout history. Women even in today's society become pregnant in hopes to win the affections of a man. Yet from generation to generation, this syndrome has proven unsuccessful, even in the lives of the faithful.

The misery of Leah has been visited in full view. The relevance of her marriage and the essence of her existence are ignored by her husband. She finally feels empowered when she gives birth to Reuben. God has seen her misery and He reacts only as He knows how.

God is so acquainted with our infirmities that He can do but one thing, and that is recompensed us for any wrong or loss. God's plan for Leah, like His plan for us is far beyond our comprehension. Leah vies for the affections and the attention of her husband. Reuben, so she thinks, will be the key. This seed is supposed to be the eye opener for Jacob to see that she is important. She wanted to prove that she was worth more than just being an object or obstacle of tradition. Many of us are giving birth to Reuben's', only to become more miserable from the ineffectiveness of our agenda. Still, out of our misery purpose is forever rearing its head. Leah was beginning a journey that would inevitably lead her to the real lover of her soul.

Most times as we are faced with the most painful circumstances and issues all we can see is the "thing" or person that the enemy is using to manipulate our emotions. The enemy desires your vision to be blurred as you go through your painful places. His job is to take full advantage of your pain and misery. Instead of Reuben serving the purpose of causing Jacob to see the importance of his fruitful wife Leah, Reuben becomes one of Leah's objects or obstacles (purpose) to win Jacob's attention, this is her only quest.

The lesson that can be learned from the first child of Leah is that when you are fruitful it is never according to your ability. God made Leah fruitful. It was God's plan that Leah not be barren. However, being emotionally tattered and torn, Leah misses the essence of her purpose. Reuben was the first child, the building block or foundation of a purposeful generation.

We should never lose sight of any vision that has been birthed. No matter how big or small, all of it works together for the good. People are moved and inspired by how man qualifies or validates them. The church suffers from the idea that you are only as important as your title or position. So, just as the world has been creative with birthing illusions of identity, the church has also.

We can see this in the workforce. There was a day when garbage collectors were called just that. Now, they are environmental technicians, and sanitation workers. As so with the church, the more important your title sounds, the more important you feel. Consequently, a title never defines the importance of the function. Don't let the enemy fake you out! Leah receives a gift not a title. This gift was given to Leah so that she could carry out the plan of God. God saw her pain, just as He sees yours. If He opened Leah's womb, He has opened yours. Stop allowing the enemy to overshadow your purpose with false illustrations. Remember he creates illusions to prevent you from seeing your true ability. Rachel was loved by Jacob; however, Leah was loved by God. He compassionately provides for her, the tools she needs to be effective, consistent and vital.

When God gifts a person with the gift to give birth to vision, they are able to duplicate it. They possess the gift of replication or reproduction. They don't just give birth to one idea and stop. They continually birth new ideas, new ventures, plans, ministries, and businesses. You are just that fruitful and do not ever forget that the enemy hates this. God has opened your womb, and just as Leah eventually discovers, you will also, that there is purpose beyond your misery.

Chapter Three

Hated by Man, Loved by God

Gen. 29:33- Then she conceived again and bore a son and said, "Because the Lord has heard that I am unloved, He has therefore given me a son also." So she named him Simeon.

The bible says that the fulfillment of the law is love (Romans 13:10). The entire work of Christ was based on God's love for His people. The very thing that Jesus died in behalf of is the very thing that we struggle with today. There is a love deficiency in the Kingdom of God. It seems as if the simplest principle of the word is the most complex commandment.

The church is the epitome of the family. Every family's success is based on the love factor. Husbands are to love their wives, as Christ loved the church and gave Himself for her (Ephesians 5:25). Children are to honor and obey their parents. Healthy family relationships produce healthy loving adults and they in turn birth healthy loving children.

Unfortunately, the church has declined in its examples of the healthy loving family. God is Love, and it is when we try to create a new design by which to love, the entire operation of love fails. The enemy from the beginning has distorted the true essence of love. Satan's whole idea was to hide the definition of love, which is God. Man's heart after the fall of Adam and Eve was deterred from Gods plan. Satan's agenda was to get man to focus on themselves, their ideals and live according to their own wills. Satan's thought was that then perhaps Gods plan of salvation would fail.

In Leah's imperfections she focuses on Jacob as her center and source of love. Because she doesn't feel adequate, she concentrates on the one that makes her feel most inadequate. That sounds strange however; most times our greatest affections are for the ones who have made us feel most uncomfortable, unloved and unwanted. There is a drive and motivation that sometimes comes from the affects of being rejected and abandoned. Somehow there is something that motivates us to pursue filling these voids by seeking the adversary that perpetrates the negative affections instead of seeking God. My biggest struggle in life was overcoming the overwhelming rejection from my father. The hidden identity of my birthright and the fact that I was unable to publicly be recognized by him as his daughter became the biggest giant to defeat in my life. Being a child born out of wedlock to a Pastor and a member of his congregation (my mother), I grew up taunted by gossips, and teased by children and adults. However, this was not as big of a problem as me not being able to be acknowledged by my father. I would never be able to wear the name of my birthright. So when my father died my entire birthright and heritage was stolen from me.

    My greatest memory was of my father's funeral. I was 10 years old and I sat on the friends' and visitors pews with my mother reading his obituary, hoping that my name would magically appear on the folded piece of paper. I remember not being able to shed a tear. All I could think about is what would happen to me now? From that day I struggled with desiring to be loved and accepted. My entire quest for life was finding my identity. I could so identify with Leah as she constantly and consistently yearned for Jacob's attention. I, myself, yearned for love and continually cleaved to my "Jacobs'."

Our "Jacobs'" can be identified as the people and things that we soul-tie ourselves to and they neither are interested in us and or they are soul-tied to others. We try to get their attention and approval, so much so, that this becomes our drive for success. We feel we can't live without their validation and approval. This spirit also creates an illusion that can drive one almost to the point of suicide because you would rather die than not receive their affection. Many of us need to denounce this spirit in our lives because until we do, we will not be able to identify or receive the true love of God because we will continually look for God in our "Jacobs".

Leah's second child Simeon was birthed under the notion that God *heard* that she was unloved. Again, she gives birth due to God's gift of fruitfulness. She is not unaware of this because she declares that **"God heard."** Still, her focus, motivation and her drive is Jacob.

As Leah, many have their affections set toward the "Jacobs'" in their lives. They know the word of God. They desire God's plan and His purpose for their lives, but they are soul-tied to those spiritual "Jacobs". Lives of many born again believers are engulfed with trying to please others more than their Savior. Some are still trying to please mothers and fathers who have rejected and neglected them. They yearn to please those who have abused them. They strive to gain the attention leaders who have overlooked and refused them. These impaired idols are monuments in their lives that causes them to birth Simeon's. God wants to heal you. He wants to cleanse you; rid, and detach you of these soul-ties. He wants to destroy and demolish those monuments of the "Jacobs'" that they have built our altars upon. Altars, since the beginning of time, were built on mounts or in conspicuous places for sacrificial offerings. People have always been rebuked by their God because of their sacrificial offerings that they have brought to the altar. The things that they have presented to God, like unclean offerings, or perhaps their motive behind their sacrifices have been questioned by God.

    The Hebrew word for altar is mez'beah which means *"to slay."* The purpose of the altar was to present a clean offering to God, to sacrifice something in behalf of something. As a desire to worship, or as a desire to be forgiven, the altar was a place of sacrifice. If we can look at this in the spiritual sense, we can identify the altars that we have built in our lives in conspicuous places in our hearts and spirits that we are sacrificing our purpose, our wills, and our emotions in behalf of. They have nothing to do with the God of our salvation. They have been built in representation to the "gods" that we have honored in our lives more than we honor the true and living God. Leah says "God heard" however, she didn't understand the great significance of the "hearing God" because her entire will was still submitted to Jacob.

God is so different from humans in that He always disregards what He sees. Humans are carnal beings and we operate more consciously according to our sensual ability. We are controlled by what we see, feel, taste and touch. Although, hearing is associated with the senses, hearing is a more complicated sensory operation. So many voices are attempting to speak to us that it can be hard to distinguish the voice of God. This is especially true, when we are governed more by our emotions than we are by God. It is amazing that we can receive signals from many different transmitters. There is our conscious voice, which is our carnal mind that speaks. This voice speaks according to what we have learned by way of experiences; good and bad. There is also the other voice coming from the enemy, this voice can work simultaneously along with the carnal voice to influence us to act according to our emotion and in conjunction with our experiences. Lastly, we have the voice of the Spirit, which speaks expressly from God. This voice has to be learned by way of the Holy Spirit's guidance and our renewing our minds according to the word of God. Unfortunately, in many cases our conscious voice, because it has not been renewed by the word, can be more powerful and we can operate in doubt. When we operate in doubt we inevitably will always follow what our conscious voice tells us. This enables the voice of the enemy to speak to our situation and circumstances to influence us to act out according to our carnal mind. God's voice, however, is supreme. There is no power higher than He. What He speaks is determined as law. Therefore, all that He may hear from us be it carnal, or influenced by an enemy that desires to destroy us, God's authority can demolish the weapons and warfare of the enemy. Isaiah 54:17- says no weapon formed against us shall prosper. It is amazing how we can quote the word and still not hear the word. We use our seeing sense. Like Leah, most of us can only appreciate what we see. If we see it we can believe it! God operates in reverse. He is moved by hearing, faith cometh by hearing and hearing by the word of God (Romans 10:17). This is why it is so important to tune out the other voices that try to speak louder than the word of God. Leah had a problem tuning out the voice of insecurity, inferiority and intimidation. When we are battling with overcoming insecurities and such, we have to walk by faith. Leah's faith in God had to become stronger than man's faith in her. The importance of her true purpose was being spoken even when she had not come to the reality of what her it meant for her.

Each time she was able to give birth she gave acknowledgement to the one who made it possible, yet she had not developed the ability to revere His plan for her life. God saw, then God heard; this is important. Our situations may not mirror the image of true success and the full purpose and plan of God may not be yet evident, however, we must know that God hears and He knows. Don't allow the enemy to consume your faith with fear. Know this; God can only perform His word. He continually puts His word above His name for our sake. Stop allowing insecurity to torment you.

Insecurity and inferiority diminishes God's ability. Although you may be capable of physically achieving certain goals, these negative characteristics can disable your productivity. Insecurity and inferiority are evil twins. They both work hand in hand to create a force between ability and the will of God for your life. When you are insecure there is no confidence in who you are and most importantly who God is. Inferiority then works on belittling purpose and the will of God for your life. Having these two alternates spirits working together to destroy and distort your vision, you are incapable of seeing the God that sees and hears all.

Another plea from Leah was that the Lord heard that she was unloved and He gave her a son. We must keep in mind that every vision and plan we birth is only because the Lord hears us. It is up to us to listen to God in return. We accomplish so much more when we ignore all of the other voices and heed to the voice of God. Nurture your vision so it can produce for you. Don't just give birth to vision and neglect it because you aren't receiving the recognition from man you feel you need. Although we are unsure about how good or bad Leah's mothering skills were there are many that neglect children out of resentment. They resent the fact that they had to sacrifice for the child. Leah could have very well resented having these children after she did not get what she needed from Jacob. How many mothers take out their frustration on their children when the fathers are inadequate? *Psalms 66:19- But certainly God has heard; He has given heed to the voice of my prayer.*

Chapter Four

A Cry for Intimacy

Gen. 29:34- She conceived again and bore a son and said; "Now this time my husband will become attached to me because I have borne Him three sons." Therefore he was named Levi.

Leah has Levi and declares that this birth will cause her husband to become attached to her. Here Leah is once again giving birth to her third child from Jacob. In Leah's striving to get Jacob's full attention she searches for a way to become intimate with him. She realizes she needs more than just for Jacob to notice her, she requires intimacy. Obviously Jacob has noticed her because he continues to impregnate her. He continues to lay with her, after all, she is his wife and he is entitled to that benefit.

As we mature intimacy in our relationships becomes vitally important. We have this yearning to find a true connection. A woman's physical make up is designed so she is a receptacle or a receiver. We are human vessels made to store, nurture and deliver. Because we are made to reproduce, we are also made to nurture what we produce. A woman's physical body is made to receive. As she attaches or connects to a male by way of physical intimacy, reproduction will naturally occur. Our mind also follows the orders of our body and the order of God's decree. This is who we are.

From the beginning the word said *"and thy desire shall be to thy husband, and he shall rule over thee"*, (Genesis 3:16). Leah could only follow the directive of her maker, God. She craved her husbands love and affection but most of all she was starving for intimacy. The above directive from God (Genesis 3:16) came only after the disobedience of Adam and Eve. Because they disobeyed God, Adam relinquishes his authority to Eve, the system of sin is born and no longer does man have dominion. He is now a carnal being susceptible to follow his own desires and no longer under God's direct safety and rule. It is important when we look at Leah and her quest for intimacy to see that although Leah may love God and may be a follower of God, she has been cursed to be led by the desires of her flesh. Her flesh desires intimacy with Jacob. She desires to be known by Jacob. She is lead by her sensual desire for her human mate. The problem with Leah, as with most is that while we become intimate with those we connect ourselves to, they sometimes do not become intimate with us.

As we look at this story we can see the difference between a male and female when it comes to intimacy. Genesis 29:10 says, "When Jacob saw Rachel…" Jacob had already based his feelings and desires on what he had already seen. The bible never states that when Leah saw Jacob that she fell in love with him. Although, when she knew Jacob, when their marriage was consummated by intercourse, her spirit was attached to him. On the contrary, Jacob's eyes had envisioned his treasure and he became engrossed with getting what he saw. There was no consummation, only a vision and he was completely convinced that Rachel was what he wanted and needed. Jacob being a visionary, led by his vision, became so overtaken with Rachel that nothing else mattered. He would go through the motions with Leah out of traditional obligation, however, his connection was with Rachel; his vision.

Sin has contaminated God's ideals for real spiritual production. To be productive we must become intimate with the source of our supply. While we crave complete intimacy, a deep understanding and a loving personal relationship; our spirits have been contaminated with a carnal perception of what we feel intimacy is. We have attached ourselves to people and things to satisfy our fleshly appetites. Once we give birth to the carnal concepts and visions that don't last and are outside of the will of God, we are again disappointed with life. Leah was again disappointed with Jacob. She was intimate with a man that could not return the same affection. Allowing him to impregnate her again and again, she is deceived by her own will and desires for intimacy. A sexual act does not define intimacy. Many have been corrupted by sexual acts and deeds that have caused them to confuse the act of sexual intercourse with true and pure intimacy. Many are sexually promiscuous, going from relationship to relationship still not filling the real true void.

Often I have wondered, in the midst of my pain, failed relationships, miscarried and aborted visions, why God never endorsed my desires at that given time. I had not realized that my desires did not line up with the will of God. We have to then admit that sometimes our desires carry an element of selfish and self-centered motives. I needed what I envisioned would fill the voids that I felt, therefore, I created my own anecdotes" due to the rejection, the need to feel accepted, validated and at last, to feel loved. Then there are visions that have been birthed from distorted views of intimacy through abusive relationships and violations. These violations steal our innocence as children most of the time. It is hard to know what true intimacy is when you have been rejected, abandoned, abused, raped or even molested. These violations can cause real distorted views of love and intimacy so much so that many will create fairy tale views of what intimacy should be. Some may even repeatedly put themselves in harm's way pursuing one dysfunctional situation after another.

An evaluation may need to be done of your life to see that some failures come from having distorted vision and views of true intimacy, and may have misconstrued the definition of real fulfillment. No matter the sacrifice, one must to come to a point of realization that we may desire to fulfill an emotional void that has very little to do with God.

Every time we give in to our wills, we give birth to our own desires. We can only give birth to what we can comprehend. Jacob was the life giver to Leah's seed. He fertilized her natural and spiritual seed. Leah could only give birth to the seed of her husband, the one she was intimate with. Her attachment was valid and lawful. Jacob was indeed her husband. For all intents and purposes he was supposed to be the object of her affection, just as he was. There was supposed to be a connection with Jacob that should have caused her to be the best that she could be as a woman, and as a wife. Jacob should have been her tent (husband) that she could dwell in (wife). Jacob's assignment was to cover, and protect her from hurt, harm and danger. By way of biblical standards, his duty would eventually be to love and cherish all that she was and all that she wasn't. But all in all, he was just filling a job position that he was not interested in being qualified for. An example of this would be, accepting a position to fulfill an immediate need until something better comes along, or until you reach your impending goal. In this case we all know what Jacob's goal was.

So Leah becomes emotionally barren but remains

tangibly fruitful. The more Jacob neglects her, the more she felt the need to fill her void with superficially giving him what she felt would win him over. Does this sound familiar? Sometimes in life, the more someone takes, the more we are willing to give. We create the diagnosis and antidote for their failed positions in our lives. When this occurs it is a sign that there is a deficit in our emotions or interference in our intimate connection with God. This deficit causes us to crave what we can physically see, touch, taste and smell. We can be so super spiritual yet cry out for human affection, lowering our spiritual standards and morals for physical pleasure and attention.

Emotions have been overpowering men and women for thousands of years. Right now there are many who can relate to where Leah was over 2000 years ago. Soul-ties and strongholds in the lives of many need to be broken from people who don't desire to know or become intimate, but only tolerate us.

Leah doesn't just fight for attention this time, she fights for intimacy. Levi was the catalyst that was supposed to initiate this bond, but she ends up with just another child birthed from Jacob. Levi's name is derived from the word lavah, which means to unite, to remain. Lavah derives from the word livyah which means something attached. We can see how Levi's name represents a stronghold in Leah's life. Do we really desire for those that are in our lives to remain? We can be sure that Leah just didn't desire for Jacob to remain, he had done this for over 7 years out of obligation. She desired a connection. Again, sexual activity is not intimacy and sexual intercourse creates strongholds and soul-ties. We know that Leah was Jacob's wife however, Jacob was Rachel's husband. This is a prime witness that just because we have gone through the motions of perpetuating certain ritual and beliefs, these things may not solidify a genuine truth. Based on Leah and Jacob's relationship their foundation initiated out of tradition and deception. Review your connections and make sure that your foundation has not been based on a foundation of deception, lies or illusions.

We enter into relationships without spiritually counting the cost. We enter into business ventures and spiritual liaisons without counting the cost. We make unwise financial decision, again without taking into consideration the detriment. It can be estimated that 90% of the failures in our lives have been because we have based those failed plans on emotional ventures. As Leah did with Jacob, we do with things and people that we give intimate permission slips into our lives. We must learn to separate intimacy from our emotions. If true communions, fellowships and connections are to be spiritually prosperous, we must learn to seek God.

Intimacy is based on true spiritual connection. Emotions are based on what our senses communicate to us according to our own needs. Be it good or bad our emotions are what we feel. That is how we confuse what is real godly intimacy with our own desires. Leah's desire for Jacob was true and correct however her emotions dictated the choices she made in her pursuit of his affections. Each time she gave birth, she did not receive even a portion of what she expected from him. *Luke 14:28-29- (amplified) For which of you, wishing to build a farm building, does not first sit down and calculate the cost [to see] whether he has sufficient means to finish it? Otherwise, when he has laid the foundation and is unable to complete (the building), all who see it will begin to mock and jeer at him.* We cannot birth or build a solid vision without proper prayer and wisdom. Emotions should not be the motivator of any vision, true intimacy should. This happens when you create an atmosphere of trust between God and yourself. Emotions create false senses of security in our desires for contentment. People will allow their emotions to minister and create emotional solutions to spiritual problems.

Leah's need was spiritual. There is no person, no thing, and no desire that can heal or fill a spiritual void. God is the instrument of true intimacy. No other connection in our lives are complete and fulfilling without the primary ingredient; the will of God. As Leah's gift of fruitfulness is utilized, she slowly comes into the realization of this.

Although Levi did not accomplish her plan, his birth defined the need for true intimacy and the fact that mere man alone cannot accomplish this difficult task. As we spend valuable time being pulled toward people and things that exhaust us, God is allowing His will to become more appealing. Leah's quest for Jacob's love, affection and attention becomes an exhausting effort for her. All of her physical and spiritual energy was being exerted by her strong will toward Jacob instead of pursuing her purpose in God. This may sound familiar to many; being physically, spiritually, and mentally drained by vices in our lives. Allowing things, circumstances, people and situations pull us further and further away from God deplete us. Our desire to be loved and accepted or our desire to be recognized and appreciated in the eyes of man can become too overwhelming. To no avail these prodigious requests and needs reveal that our true hidden longing is for pure intimacy.

Levi's birth seems ineffective, and Leah does not get what she desires from Jacob, it brings her face to face with her real issue. As she experiences inconsistency and lack of attention so frequently that the disappointment pushes her closer and closer to God. Consequently, it is our experiences with our Jacobs' that lead us closer and closer to God. We should fear the Lord and reverence the word long before calamity breaks us, but it is a known fact that in most peoples' lives it is misfortune and disappointment that draw them closer to God. When all else fails we find God. When there is no true pure connection with a physical being who sees the real us, we search for God. In our most depressed and dead states we find God. It is not until we exhaust all measures and we have used up all of our carnal resources that we turn to a God that knows exactly how to love us. We crave pure love. Love without conditions is what we as a people truly need. That is why it is so easy to be inundated and infatuated with a lover and then all of a sudden the momentum wears off and again you instantly, in a second know that something is missing. We suffer with deficiencies in our emotions that lead us on a perpetual journey, searching for the missing link; true love. Not only does this apply to relationships, it can relate to careers, the quest for validation, approval or even power, due to feeling like we have never had control. Having no identity in anything in life, moving from one project to another and never being happy for any definitive period of time is a sign of a void of true fulfillment. The enemy always creates a diversion to keep you continually seeking and never finding what you feel will make you happy or satisfied. You don't need another relationship, you don't need another ministry or church home, you may not need another career to erase the season of lack or the dry place that you are in. You need to realize that you need a connection with God! Voids, dry places, and ineffective seasons are a derivative of a lack of intimacy with the Father. Whenever we are so connected to things that frustrate us instead of empower us, we have missed God somewhere. The sad part is that we continue to build our visions, our relationships and everything else without even noticing that we are frustrated and keep failing because ultimately there is no intimacy with the Father. ***Psalms 127:1- Unless the LORD builds the house, they labor in vain who build it...***

Every vision requires the builder to have an intimate relationship with God first. Focus is lost in an attempt is to form intimacy with the tangible instead of the spiritual. This could have very well been Leah's story as she tried time and time again to find the next best thing to get Jacob's attention. She created in her mind all the things that she felt would cause Jacob to desire her. In essence the very things that she felt would draw Jacob were the things that God was using to draw her. Leah's need is what drew her to God. Your need, your misfortune, your inability to be whatever it is you feel you need to be, is what will draw you to God. If it hasn't, let it draw you today. True and pure intimacy is calling and it is what will speak to the elements in your life and cause them to line up with the will of God. It is time to stop shedding tears over failed relationships and seemingly failed businesses, visions and ministries. This is the hour to cry out for true intimacy to the point that failure is no longer an option and this intimacy births the will of God and His desire for your life.

Chapter Five

A Purpose Birthed Praise...This Time

Gen. 29:35- Once again Leah became pregnant and gave birth to another son. She named him Judah, for she said; "Now I will praise the Lord!" And she stopped having children.

Let's look at Leah's life and see just how a situation such as hers can be called destiny. The state of her affairs is actually known from the very minute that Laban agrees with Jacob to give Rachel, his youngest daughter's hand in marriage. Leah, Jacob, or Rachel has no idea of the events that would take place to alter the original agreement. We can interpret this because everything that took place on the wedding day was done in accordance with Laban's agreement to give Rachel to Jacob and not Leah. When Jacob completes his seven years of service, he then asks Laban for "his wife" Rachel. *Gen. 29:20-21- So Jacob served seven years for Rachel and they seemed to him but a few days because of his love for her. Then Jacob said to Laban, "**Give me my wife**, for* *my time is completed, that I may go in to her."* Laban then has a marriage feast for Jacob and supposedly Rachel, however, he then sends Leah in to Jacob.

    The enemy has a plan for our lives that we know not. We can be minding our own business, going about our day enjoying Jesus and then he rears his ugly head in our situations. It happens so fast that we have to really go back in our minds to pinpoint his entry. No doubt this is what occurred with Leah. When this story is viewed by theologians most of the emphasis is put on Jacob, as he was an heir and seed of Abraham. Needless to say, Leah is a very noteworthy and vital asset in the life of Jacob. Although she was thrown into a hostile situation so she does the best she knows how to adapt to her environment.

    Women have the wonderful gift of knowing how to improvise. We know how to substitute to the point that we can make a void element look like something. Leah in her own way does this. She doesn't have to, but because she desires so much to be loved by her husband she creates a new vision and mission with every new birth. Leah doesn't realize that God has given her the ability to reproduce to be used for him only. God opened her womb because *"he saw she was hated"* (Gen. 29:31). If we look over the course of our lives how many babies natural as well as spiritual that have we birthed out of our emotional struggle?

Leah births Reuben first. Her vision was that *"God saw" her misery* and that this birth would now cause Jacob to love her. This didn't happen according to how she saw it. Next she gives birth to Simeon, and she envisions *that "God heard she was unloved"* and because of this birth, her husband would now love her. Again, Leah is speaking amiss because this does not sway Jacob in the least. Leah then gives birth to Levi, desiring more than love this time, she realizes that intimacy is what she needs, *"this time my husband will be attached to me."* All three births even though they do not accomplish her set goals, lead her to discover her real true purpose.

Using slang from our time we would call Leah a sucker, or say that she was foolish for chasing Jacob as she did. After giving birth to three of his babies, still to no avail Jacob loves Rachel and Leah still needs love. We all have had similar experiences in life. We were starving for love and affection and running after the wrong individual to fulfill that desire. Leah wasn't completely wrong, as Jacob was her husband. Jacob wasn't completely wrong in that he loved his wife Rachel. After all, Rachel was Jacob's vision and purpose. He worked 7 years to have her and dedicated another seven years to fulfill an obligation that would ensure that Rachel would be his. Before the marriage was consummated, after the initial seven years, when he approached Laban, he stated, *"Give me my wife for my time is completed (Gen. 29:21)."* He had already resolved in his heart that Rachel was his wife. Leah and Jacob were both thrown into a relationship out of wrong motives. So they both cope the best way they know how. Leah does not know how to go through the motions as most women don't once they are connected to a man. Here she was given to a man that had no desire for her, this man unknowingly has lain with her, and now she is soul-tied to him while he has a vision for someone else. From that point on she chases Jacob's love. She woos him hoping that birthing his babies will win his affection and attention. She begs him for intimacy and now she is tired.

There is a point in everyone's life when they not only get physically tired but spiritually tired. We make decisions, we create relationships, and we direct our energies to so many projects that have been birthed out of mere emotional starvation. These actions wear us out to the point of saying, "God I can't take any more!" Some of us have been right at the brink of giving up. Our affections and emotions have been pulled into the direction of things and people and not God. We then make it to the point of saying, "enough is enough." This is when our Jacob's become obsolete. Our only desire is to find out where God is. We start praying for His will to be done in our lives. We start seeking His face and not His hand. We then seek to create and birth intimacy with Him. At this end we see God at His best in our situations.

All of us possess attributes of Leah at some point in our lives. As Christians we can sometimes be so judgmental of each other when we are going through rough seasons in life. We try to analyze how we would react in another person's situation but we never see God. Everyone fails a test every now and then. Leah definitely could have felt like she was a failure after all she had been through.

What can be admired about Leah is that she does not give up. She doesn't fade out of the picture. She doesn't die out of the story as an insignificant wife that Jacob never wanted. The bible goes on to say that, *"she conceived again..."* (Gen. 29:35). What was going to be different about this birth? The devil loves to mess with purpose when he feels he has caused us to make bad decisions. He reminds us of all of our failed ventures, businesses, ministries, and relationships. We must possess the same tenacity as Leah, and don't give up. Give birth again!

Again Leah conceives and she bore a son and said, *"This time I will praise the Lord (Gen. 29:35)."* When the enemy wants to speak to you about the birth of this vision, tell him that, "This time it's praise!" It's not being birthed for Jacob, or for any voids that need to be filled in your life. You are not trying to get attention or affection. You don't need notoriety or justification. You have just decided that it is time for Praise to be birthed. Leah's focus is no longer Jacob. Her desire is now to give birth to something that will signify the purpose of God in her life. The scripture says that she stopped bearing children after this. The birth of Judah was a witness that God finally fulfilled His purpose in her life. She was no longer needy, intimidated or inferior. She realizes that it was God all along that she needed.

We never know how Leah's and Jacob's relationship went after this although we can see that she and Rachel remained as his wives, but what we do know is that Leah no longer needed to feel validated. She realized that she was blessed. God blessed her with the ability to give birth. She had the gift of fruitfulness. Leah gives definition to her gift and she calls him ***Judah*** or Praise. This is what God is looking for out of our lives. Your greatest ability is to give anything that you birth; visions, ministries, businesses, relationships, let them all be defined as ***PRAISE***.

Judah was a declaration, an affirmation and a confession. Through his birth she confesses to God that she now understands that her life is not defined by what man thinks or feels. In fact, God has given everyone diverse abilities to give birth to Judah. There is no need for a barren lifestyle. Rachel was physically barren; however, because of life's circumstances Leah was spiritually barren. Surprisingly, what we produce by way of the spirit is what matters most to God. All of your physical abilities come from Him so that you can deliver spiritual results. This is done by putting what we are able to do in the flesh to work for God.

I minister to leaders frequently and what I have noticed over the years is how so many leaders in ministry use the ministry as a source to validate their carnal power. Many are given the idea that power comes from position, education, carnal wisdom, etc. So what we see in ministry in some cases are people stepping into leadership positions because they feel the need to be validated or to gain the acceptance they never received. They may feel the need to prove the point that they are successful to those who have rejected them. These people fail again and again at building anything effective. As afore mentioned they can never stay the course on any one thing. They don't weather the storm and can never stand the test of time. Sometimes proven by years of stagnation and frustration these people go in continual circles. This doesn't mean that they aren't called or chosen, it means that they do not yet know who they are inwardly by way of God's spiritual justification. They haven't discovered their true identity and purpose. Leah was this type of person for a moment. She did not know who she was. She came into a hostile situation and the enemy began to pour on the spirit of rejection and intimidation. She began to see herself through Jacob's eyes, as not being sufficient enough. So she performs and functions subconsciously from his perception of her. Our biggest adversity is when we began to see ourselves through the eyes of others.

This time though, Leah stands, takes off the blinders and becomes volatile. Leah doesn't waddle in self pity. She doesn't mourn over the fact that she has done all she can do and still she doesn't win Jacob over. She doesn't crawl into hole of depression, but she gives birth again! This may sound crazy however, just because we have made mistakes or missed some instructions through the process of birthing visions, doesn't mean that we just quit. Any visionary that has become great did not do so over night. They had many setbacks and disappointments. They have made many mistakes and have missed God due to their emotions and making impromptu decisions, but they kept going.

Nothing is ever easy when we are called to give birth to purpose. Birthing Judah may be the hardest labor and delivery there is. It is even harder when we don't have the assistance of a skilled physician or midwife. Leah's first three births were ill assisted births. She travailed on her own. She had no proper or skilled birthing coach. When we allow those who are not anointed for our lives dictate to us during our birthing process we are attempting to give birth with inexperienced assistance. Notice that everyone has all of these remedies and suggestions when you are with child or expecting. Some even claim to know how to determine the sex of the baby from the way a mother's womb is positioned when she is carrying the baby. They may even be correct in their assessments purely by luck or maybe from experience. In spite of this, we must realize that it is the anointing and wisdom of God that speaks to us when we are in a birthing position, to ensure an effective and easy delivery. Leah's agenda to give birth for the approval of Jacob may have seemed unsuccessful in her eyes. She no doubt felt worse after each of these births and Jacob's attention and affection still remained constant toward Rachel.

    When Leah births Judah, she births the true plan of God. She births Judah with the mindset that God will receive all the praise from the birth of that child, Judah. It must be understood that the births of Reuben, Simeon and Levi were not meaningless. Those births gave way for the purpose of God to be revealed in Leah's life. You may feel that the visions you have birthed over the years that weren't successful or that did not grow, such as; failed and premature ministries, failed relationships and unsuccessful business ventures were not the will of God. Inadvertently, from the births of those visions, you learned how to trust God more. You were able to see what you should and should not have done. Each baby that I gave birth to taught me better parenting skills. I learned what worked as a mother and what didn't. All in all, every baby Leah delivered prepared her for her true destiny; giving birth to Judah.

Let's look at the definition of Judah. Judah is another definition of praise. Praise can take on different connotations and characteristics. One definition is **barak** which defines an action. Barak means to bless or pronounce good things upon a recipient. *Halal* is another form of praise, which defines boasting or exulting. *Yada* defines a true confession of praise. Out of yada, *todah* is birthed, in which the name Judah derives from.

Judah can be seen as Leah's testimony. Out of all she had been through, Leah could have imagined life to be a bitter cycle of failures. Truly Leah was able to pronounce, boast, and confess the good of God through the birth of Judah. No doubt she could have well been justified to see her failures, as she experienced rejection over and over again. If we look at our own lives we can find some of our greatest miracles deriving from our greatest miseries. Ill circumstances and issues have a way of grooming us for the future. We all may suffer similar challenges however, we may respond differently to these challenges and unfavorable circumstances in life. We can look at those that have been abused and we can see that every person has a different response or reaction to the circumstances they have suffered. Some victims become perpetrators of the same acts they have suffered. Remember that saying; "hurting people hurt people", and in a lot of instances this is a true statement. Some take the extreme right approach and may become passive and revert to not exercising any type of authority. They may continue to be victims. This may show up in the form of not exercising authority in disciplining their own children, or by simply by not taking control of their own lives and destinies. Then there are those that choose not to quit pursuing their purpose, they are relentless; they are the **Leahs'**. The abuse and rejection that they have suffered pushes them closer to God. They realize that there is something that God is trying to get out of them and no matter how many failed visions, unsuccessful relationships and carnal ideas that they have birthed, they keep seeking for the true essence of God and purpose in their lives. All that they have gone through has only prepared them for Judah.

Judah became just that for Leah, a real praise report. Judah was a testimony of the fact that Jacob was no longer a stronghold in her life. She was no longer bound hand and foot by their fruitless relationship. Her need had finally pushed her to the real lover of her soul, God. Leah does away with the victim mentality and realizes just how much God loves her. She discovers her true beauty and true purpose this time. She gives birth to Praise.

God uses Jacob, one of the heirs of promise, to impregnate a woman that many could look at as irrelevant, to give birth to one of the most important seeds that would carry the bloodline of our Savior Jesus Christ. Why then, didn't God use Rachel to birth Judah? It would have made for a better story; the woman that Jacob was madly in love with births Judah who inadvertently was tied to the lineage of Christ. Out of all that Jacob would have gone through to get Rachel, and then they would birth the seed of purpose and praise! Yes, that would have made for better reading. But God in His infinite power seems to always use those who seem powerless or impoverished to man to prove he can get the praise and the glory from weakened defeated vessels. Leah was the perfect woman for this assignment. She was the ideal protégé to be used to birth a seed of such vital importance. Her insignificance, her state of disdain, the rejection she suffered, shined a supernatural light on her and God said, "I must use her." If we could just catch the revelation in this, our lives can be revolutionized by a powerful story of a woman who seemed worthless in all aspects, nevertheless, was used for God's purpose. Those of you who have felt worthless, suffered much abuse, rejected, abandoned and misuse have been empowered like Leah. Leah's testimony is, ***"Devil, you lose! This time I'm giving birth to Judah (Praise)."***

Chapter Six

The Importance of the Judah Assignment

Genesis 49:8-9- Judah your brothers will praise you; your hand will be on the neck of your enemies; your father's sons will bow down to you. You are a lion's cub, Judah; you return from the prey, my son. Like a lion he crouches and lies down, like a lioness—who dares to rouse him? (New International Version)

In view of Leah's life it is important to see all aspects of God at work. We can not allow the enemy to overwhelm us with life's circumstances. When we allow this we underestimate the miracles that God is working in our lives daily. Leah's life is a miracle in itself. She daily overcomes obstacles that could have very well crippled her spiritually and emotionally. It does not go to say that she did not experience emotional lows. All of us, at some point in our lives will face emotional lows that may seem almost impossible to conquer. However, when God has an assignment and task for us, we will inevitably complete it. When I look at my life and the challenges that I have faced on so many levels, I am amazed at how far God has brought me. I am a woman who was a broken and emotional mess whom God saw fit to transform for His purpose.

Leah's life was purposed for Praise (Judah). No matter what journey life's trials had taken her on, God was at work even in her most desperate moments. You may sometimes become desperate to reach your goals and accomplish your missions. Your lives, at times don't measure up to the visions and missions that God has set before you. Therefore, the enemy creates continual diversions to try to overthrow the plan and will of God for your lives. Just know that they are only diversions and illusions.

You were commanded to be fruitful and multiply. This is your weapon. This weapon is such a great force that every time you are impregnated the enemy wars to kill the baby (vision, purpose, or dream). Leah's rejection was not about what Jacob was or wasn't doing. The rejection was apart of the enemy's plan to steal purpose and ultimately kill Praise (Judah). This is important to see, because we must realize that God never blesses, anoints or empowers what He can't get glory out of, and the enemy only wars against those he is threatened by.

Leah is one of the first women whom God empowers to give birth, as well as, she was the carrier of the seed and lineage of our savior Jesus Christ. Judah was the purposed child. God had Leah in mind from the beginning. Her assignment was orchestrated by the most High. Every one of our lives has blueprints assigned and designed by God. We are chosen for specific purposes in specified seasons. Leah's description as being the oldest sister with "lazy eyes" by man, but she was God's chosen vessel to birth Praise. Everything that God anoints us to do must have the seal of praise on it. It is not our glory that should be attributed to the gifts, talents and visions that we are blessed with. It is God's glory that should be seen when the manifestations of these plans are unleashed in the earth.

There are No Insignificant Births

1 Chronicles 5:2- and through Judah was the strongest of his brothers and a ruler come from him, the rights of the firstborn belonged to Joseph...

God opens Leah's womb for the purpose of giving birth to Praise, then again, she has three babies before she births and understands her true purpose. Reuben was the first born son of Leah. Although Reuben grew up with his own character inconsistencies, he still inherits the rights of the first born. The visions that you have birthed, although they have seemingly not been fruitful or may have even failed, they have all been incentives to get your real purpose; Praise into the earth. It is the births of the former things that prepare us for the birth of great things. It is failure that has driven the most effective men of God, millionaires, entrepreneurs and the like to their greatest level of success. They learn to mark their failures and experiences. They review their inconsistencies and they plan for fruitful futures.

Leah understands her inconsistency in birthing visions with emotional agendas attached, and because of this she was inspired to seek God for true fulfillment. She knew she was purposed to give birth. Giving birth was Leah's destiny.

In my worse seasons, I knew I was anointed to lead. As discouraged as I was at times, God continually birthed vision in me. He consistently reminded me of what my true purpose was. God never looked at my present state, He always allowed me to see the greatness that was going to be birthed out of me. Some days I felt like a mother long over due. I was carrying a baby pass full term. I was frustrated because I just wanted the baby out of me! However, God was saying, "I am going to allow you to carry this ministry until you are prepared to give birth!" What I found out was that it was not God that was delaying me; it was my not being prepared for greatness that had me long overdue. God knew Leah needed time to set her affections toward Him before He could allow Judah to come forth. The environment and the atmosphere had to be conducive for perfected Praise.

Rev. 12:4- [4] Its tail swept a third of the stars out of the sky and flung them to the earth. The dragon stood in front of the woman who was about to give birth, so that it might devour her child the moment he was born.

The initial impartation I received from God was the impartation to minister to women. When God anointed me for this ministry I was at a stage in my life where I was weary of producing anything without real purpose. There were women's ministries being birthed all over the nation. There were conferences going on monthly and I couldn't, for the life of me, understand why there would be a need for another women's ministry. I began to ask God why, and even more so, I questioned the need for another women's ministry. I was tired of attending conferences sensationalized by inspiring Christian rhetoric, yet no change occurring. Cookie cutter women's ministries were appearing all over the place, one after the other, with savvy names and seemingly big conferences with well named ministers. Yet birthing no change or purpose for those who truly needed it. I would see the same women at these events many attending for another quick fix or pursuing an emotional high. They were seeking another new revelation or word that would magically transform their present situation. What was most discouraging was the fact that the majority of those who attended these conferences would be Christian women who were already in leadership. I would wonder what would be the purpose. Shouldn't they already be inspired and empowered enough to reach those who really needed help? All the same, my heart was bleeding for the Leahs' that were being rejected, thrown away and overlooked. My heart's desire was to be able to share with hurting and neglected women that didn't realize their travail came from carrying a long over due Judah (Praise). I was longing to be a midwife who could assist them with their delivery.

God began speaking to me profoundly about the need for genuine women's ministry. He began to show me that there were not enough midwives that specialized in problem and high risk pregnancies and deliveries. From the beginning of time babies, especially the male child, has been sought out by assassins. The enemy's desire is to kill or abort anything that will bring God total and ultimate Praise. The serpent expected Adam and Eve's disobedience to abort or kill the plan of God for their lives and their seed. Although God did reverse His covenant benefits He still initiated a plan to restore man's total fellowship with Him.

Women have such a precious gift. There is not a Pastor, Prophet, or billionaire that did not come from the womb of a woman. Every great gift that has ever transformed or revolutionized worlds and nations were birthed by women. We carry purpose, we birth great visions, and we nurture the gifts of God that are ordained to bring great visions to pass. We may feel unworthy or even unequipped to give birth to the plan and will of God. Most new mothers go through the state of being overwhelmed and worrying if they will be a good mother. In all truthfulness, once we give birth, mothers are graced with a natural ability to nurture our seed.

When God was calling me into full-time leadership I felt so overwhelmed. I was continually asking God if I would ever be worthy enough. Still, I was pregnant and inevitably ready to give birth. As far as God was concerned I was long over due. I can remember fighting with God and feeling the baby (vision) kicking in me. All at the same time, just as a woman that is in the birthing position and the baby is positioning its way down the birthing canal, the labor gets almost unbearable, and sometimes we want to stop pushing. We are tired, out of strength, breathless and a lot of times we say, "I can't do this anymore!" However, the midwife or physician and nurses are there saying, "you can do this, just one more push and you are there!" When I truly began to seek God for strength and direction in order to give birth to this vision that was much bigger than I had even conceived, I could finally hear God saying, "just one more push!" In other words He was saying to me, whether or not you desire it, this baby is coming and the quicker you position yourself and push, the easier the delivery will be. I am saying to you all who are struggling, just one more push!

    This generation is what I call the "microwave generation." They desire everything within minimal processing time. The less time it takes to make things materialize, the better. Many are going through the motions and are using a generic god instead of the brand name God, the savior. We can't afford Him, so we buy the superficial or a knock off that looks like His work, however, it isn't. I compare some of our relationships with God to the movie Pretty Woman with Julia Roberts and Richard Gere. Although Julia was a call girl, she had certain rules that she would play by when dealing with her clients. Her rule was never to kiss while performing. She didn't mind the sexual intercourse as long as she didn't have to kiss. Kissing to her represented real and true intimacy which opened her up to being vulnerable. So she gave her clients a quick fix and she was paid for her services and there was no attachment. Some of us have formed this same alliance with God. We desire to reap the benefits without any true attachment or intimacy. With the attachment baby Simeon, Leah required intimacy, and this requires giving of ones entire self which eventually causes travail. Any relationship where real intimacy is attained travail and warfare is certain. No God ordained relationship is birthed without it. Your relationship with God will not be fruitful without travail and warfare. Stop trying to get out of the stirrups and push!

True vision and purpose are in no way microwaveable nor do they manifest without labor. If anyone is wondering when you will give birth to the Praise that God has ordained for your life, it will be when you commit yourself to embracing this concept. Judah was not the first, second or third child because Leah had to first be broken enough to even conceive what God had ordained for her even from her humble beginnings. She had to go through the motions of trying to perform for man and being broken in the process of not receiving the essence of her true worth to really see what God had blessed her with. When she saw God she stopped giving birth out of desperation. God doesn't anoint visions and assignment of desperation. He can only anoint the genuine.

Judah is important to your assignment because Judah is birthed out of a pure commitment and worship to God. Our visions have to be free of our agendas and our motives in order to give birth to pure unadulterated praise.

God is pushing you to birth Praise. You cannot be hindered or delayed. You have not been denied. I am speaking into your spirit that there will be no failed ministry and no aborted vision. No mingled relationship, childhood abuse, rejection or even the spirit of intimidation can keep you from birthing Judah. You are a modern day Leah, inwardly beautiful and blessed by God. You are favored over others and your life has been chosen to show forth God's praises.

Chapter 7

Avoiding Emotional Pitfalls & Setbacks

Being pregnant is a serious condition. One should be very cautious when it comes to carrying a child. Medical science says that a major cause of death is childbirth. Many have died during childbirth. I would hear my mother and others speak of a condition call a "setback". Most women who gave birth in my day did not go out until after 6 weeks once they have given birth. I can remember my mother demanding me to stay inside after the birth of my first daughter because she didn't want me to have a "setback". True enough, many women who have not followed the guidelines of proper care and safety after giving birth, and return quickly to their normal way of life, going out and among people, have suffered major conditions that have sometimes even put them back in the hospital. This was due to their immune systems not being repaired and restored enough to handle everyday environments and fight airborne viruses and infections that were contagious.

I want to address a few practical lessons that I have learned along the way. Giving birth to vision is being viewed just like giving birth to a baby. New mothers have to learn parenting skills. Usually we find out that we are pregnant long before it is time for us to give birth. So we have time to read study and physically prepare ourselves for carrying the baby (vision). The first thing the physician does is lets us know what trimester we are in. He then gives us a prescription for pre-natal vitamins, and if it is our first baby, we sometimes receive literature that explains the entire process of what we will experience while carrying the baby. When I knew that I was to lead, God gave me specific instructions about how to carry out the vision. I have seen many people who give birth prematurely because they do not follow the orders of the physician. They refuse to wait on the manifestation of the vision. Just because God gives you a vision doesn't mean that it is the time or the season for it to be birthed. Proper preparation and nurturing is required to give birth to a healthy vision.

All in all, I heard the voice of God regarding my call. He then spoke to me and said, "just as it takes 9 months to give birth to a healthy baby, it will take a certain amount of time to nurture and give birth to a healthy vision. God then began to give instructions in order to ensure a healthy delivery. I didn't immediately run and find a building. I began to prepare myself spiritually and naturally for the call. I went back to school. I began to develop the ministry vision and mission. Ministry corporation documents and bylaws were initiated and all of the foundational things that were needed to validate the ministry were set in order. My many years of serving and observing ministry pitfalls and miscarriages prepared me for giving birth to a healthy vision. Another thing that God allowed me to see from a natural standpoint was that no baby comes out fully grown and developed. Babies have to grow. Visions have to grow. Businesses have to grow. Defeat the enemy that desires you to set your sights on becoming big overnight. There are really no overnight successes. If there are, they miss a lot of the growth processes and are spiritually premature. I had to fight the enemy of desiring to be big instead of being effective. I developed a well grounded view of what could be expected in ministry so there would be no turning around. There would be no troubled moments that would come to cause me to abort the mission. I learned to embrace the Braxton Hicks and realize that they were just false labor pains. I learned how to grow in trimesters. I didn't try to launch a full fledge ministry without the provision and the assistance.

Usually when we see our visions, we see them at their mature stages. If we are not careful we are discouraged when we are not overnight successes or the ministry has not grown as fast as we expected or the business has not turned over the profits that we thought, in the time that we expected it to. We have to remember that our visions, businesses and dreams have to grow into the mega ministries, businesses and dreams that we envision from the beginning. Babies have to learn to walk, talk and feed themselves but all of this occurs in stages, not overnight.

We must be careful even after we have given birth to our visions not to entangle ourselves in certain environments and affairs that will cause us to have a setback. We also want to protect our vision in the infancy stages. Infants are prone to a condition called SIDS or Sudden Infant Death Syndrome. This is the same with your vision. Demonic warfare is assigned to kill your baby once it is birthed. Be watchful and vigilant as you protect and nurture your new baby.

Our children go through the stages of being very impressionable. When I put my first daughter into daycare, as she began to interact with other children she began to pick up some of their habits and ways of doing things. I was shocked when she came home one day and I told her that she couldn't have something she wanted and she threw her first temper tantrum, kicking and screaming. I had to remember that she was in an environment where she could pick up many habits, good and bad. Still it was my position as her parent to teach her the proper way to communicate and respond. This will be the same with you. Your vision is unlike any other. Avoid the urge to copy cat or be persuaded by your peers to implement things into your vision that God has not ordained. Protect and nurture your baby. Groom them for success.

Being a woman I had to battle with my emotions as well as society's view of women in leadership positions. I grew up in a denomination that has never embraced women in formative and leadership positions in the church until recently. I had to battle in my own mind regarding the call on my life.

I've been able to see ministry from both sides of the coin when dealing with gender biases in the church. To be able to address this issue I would like to share one of my experiences with you.

Our ministry once had the pleasure of visiting with a ministry outside of our denomination. Myself as the visionary was very excited about the invite. To me it was a sign of religious barriers being broken between denominations. I wasn't the speaker that was requested, this denomination has yet to fully embrace women in leadership, yet and still I was excited about the open door that had been extended. When the service began, all the preliminaries had to be done. The acknowledgement of the leaders was extended. Surely, the Pastor knew that I was there, however I was not acknowledged. The pastor from my ministry tried to make my presence known and I humbly signaled to advise him that it was okay and I needed no acknowledgement. My presence being known was not the important factor; it was that we received an open invitation to share the Gospel with our brethren. My prayer has always been answered in reference to our ministry that wherever God allows us to go, that revival takes place. So the entire time, I'm sitting waiting in expectation of what God was getting ready to do. I knew that God was surely about to move in that service. Sure enough the pastor ignited a fire in that place that could not be extinguished. The presence of the Lord, worship and healing was taking place. I humbly assisted in the altar service; I assisted with prayer, never trying to make my presence known.

On the contrary, it seems as if the enemy loves to rare his head, when God is doing a work. The altar service is then transformed into a circus act when two other women who are known to be leaders invite themselves to the altar to pray and lay hands on the people. As the pastor in charge began to pray with the leader of that ministry, one of the women proceeded to the pulpit to assist with the prayer, already aware that this denomination did not share their pulpit with women. I was both grieved and embarrassed. The entire time I am thinking that the Holy Spirit is being grieved, there is no order and God is definitely not in this open show of unsanctioned authority. Obviously, they were out of order. They were not apart of the ministry team that was in charge, nor were they invited to engage in the service. First, the bible says in *1 Cor. 14:32-33* *[32] The spirits of prophets are subject to the control of prophets. For God is not a God of confusion but of peace, as in all the churches of the saints*. Then it dawned on me; could this be a reason that women are not respected in ministry? There are some very important things that I would like to submit regarding effective leadership for women:

- Our leadership ability should always come from a place of humility. Deborah was a prophet and a judge

(Judges 4:4-5), however, she preferred to judge silently from behind the scenes realizing that because she was already called to a hostile position as a woman, she needed to be wise about her approach so that her office and work could be both respected and effective.

Judges 4:9-[9]And she said, I will surely go with you; nevertheless, the trip you take will not be for your glory, for the Lord will sell Sisera into the hand of a woman. And Deborah arose and went with Barak to Kedesh.

- Our leadership is based on our ability and character and not our title. We should never be offended if we are not acknowledged. When we are confident in our identity and the work that God has called us to we will never fight for notoriety or position. ***Romans 8:30-And those he predestined, he also called; those he called, he also justified; those he justified, he also glorified.***

I have witnessed women who have become bitter and hostile toward men and it shows in their leadership.

This brings me to another point; I was asked what I thought about women carrying the title as a Bishop. Now, because I do have my own opinion, I try to keep an open mind when it comes to my sisters in ministry. So, I answered as wisely as I knew how. Since I choose the Apostolic view of things I will quote Paul; ***Ephesians 4:1-I therefore, the prisoner of the Lord, beseech you that ye walk worthy of the vocation wherewith ye are called…***

Our lives are divinely called to a spiritual order, and this is our vocation. Nevertheless, it must completely line up with the word of God. My personal opinion, and we all have one, is that I am not concerned with the office or even the title, my concern is how we walk in the office and or the title. I am a woman by my very nature as well as my character. I lead with authority, yet I am humble enough to submit to my brethren in the Gospel.

Steve Harvey recently wrote a book, "Act Like a Lady and Think Like a Man." The problem comes in when we take on the latter part of Steve Harvey's ideal, *"think like a man"*. I have witnessed the nature of women changing with the offices and titles they take on. I inquired from the individual I was speaking with regarding his thoughts on women carrying the title of Bishop. I could relate with his experience with women in certain roles. I am a sister, and just as this brother, I have witnessed women who have become hardened, effeminate, male bashers. This has always been a concern to me in leadership. Our first vocation or call is that of a woman. Proverbs 31 gives us a wonderful model of a woman in leadership in her home and abroad. If we can't submit to each other, how can we say that we are submitted to God? If our titles have caused us to become masculine and embittered against the very blueprint we were formed from (Adam), where is God in our vocation? We have to avoid certain pitfalls so that our ministries as women can be effective.

Leah's effectiveness came from the ability God anointed her with. She was a woman whom God had blessed with a fruitful womb. Had she neglected her first ministry as a woman, God could have never birthed Judah. We have to realize that we do not have to harden our identities in order to be effective in leadership positions.

The world gives us a distorted view of ministry as women. I believe that because we have been suppressed, abused and neglected in so many areas that we adapt this survival mentality and we ultimately began to fight and defend our positions and callings when there is no need for that. The most effective leaders are the ones who know who they are and are not threatened by others perceptions. People's thoughts' about our gender and our call doesn't sway us or cause us to become bitter. We operate as women without being defensive and emotional.

The worse thing that could occur in leadership for a woman is when they lead according to their emotions. Leah was empowered from the beginning to birth purpose however; her emotions lead her to make impaired decisions. Therefore, she gave birth to her plan instead of God's plan. This can be a setback. God can lead you to birth a vision; however, if you neglect to carry out the plan precisely as He has designed it we will have many setbacks and delays.

God has given me an eye to really see and discern those operating in ministry beyond the natural. In my early years of ministry I admired women in leadership who were able to be effective in what they were called to do and that were carrying out the plan of God in the spirit of excellence. My desire was to also be able to operate in ministry and be confident that it was God that was leading me. I recall attending the service of one of my favorite leading ladies. I always enjoyed going to her services because she always lead and operated in such a spirit of excellence. As I was sitting in the service God began to deal with me. It was as if I was at a panoramic movie show. Everyone was seemingly worshipping. As she was praying for people they were receiving their impartation, yet the spirit of God revealed that they were all just going through the motions. He said to me that this woman of God had been given specific instructions for her ministry and that He had desired to shift her to another level however, she had refused to do what He had instructed. In not following the complete plan of God and shifting when the season had come, He could no longer endorse ministry on that level.

As we are growing and our visions are being nurtured for maturity we must listen to God for explicit instructions. This ministry was a ministry that operated according to the five fold ministry gifts. The woman of God had a strong prophetic mantle and people were drawn to her because of the prophetic gift and anointing that was on her life. However, God was requiring her to go to another level. We must realize that in all that we do, whether it is ministry or business, or any other birthed vision; our babies require a healthy diet. As the baby grows it can not just survive off of formula, it will require the introduction of solid foods to continue to grow properly. What works for an infant will not work for a toddler. As the baby grows they require development at each stage of growth. This is the same with vision. If your vision is to be consistently effective and successful, what you do in one season may not be what you need to do in the next.

  Prophecy is just one of the gifts that are needed in the church. However, the word is the foundation of a strong vision. We must know how to incorporate a balanced diet for our visions. I believe that because prophecy was drawing the people she continued to do what would draw the people and did not shift when God instructed her to do so. So the people were still coming, the ministry was filled with those desiring the prophetic, however the essence of God's spirit was no longer moving in signs and wonders. In this case, God will always do what He needs to do for His people, that doesn't necessarily mean that we are operating in the totality of God's will. This is indicative to seeing people go to a certain level and they can go no further. When we experience stagnation, we need to realize that we have dropped the ball in the process and we must trace our steps back towards the will of God and pick up where He left off at.

Your vision and purpose must have the *Judah* endorsement. There will always be areas that require improvement. There will be times when you really have to seek the face of God for His direction. Your assignment will require you to operate in faith on an entirely different level as God increases and advances you. You will not be able to depend on the validation of man. In fact, most times others will not be able to comprehend what God is doing in your life, when it is He who is at work. Allow God to minister to you as you birth Judah in this season. He is going beyond your broken places and ministering to your true essence. He has opened your womb, and you must give birth to true and pure and perfected Praise!

Judah's Prayer

Father God, I pray that as every person has read this book that it has ministered to the essence of their being. I pray that your anointing is saturating their hearts and minds and revealing unto them their true inner beauty and call to your work. I bind every spirit of inferiority, intimidation, and rejection. They are set free and delivered from word curses, abuse, be it physical, emotional and verbal that has long attached itself to their spirit and that has created altars and strongholds in their lives. Strongholds and soul-ties are being broken right now off of their minds and their bodies. They are being released in Jesus Name. Their hearts are being totally and completely healed from hurt. They are being released from the shame of their past. I speak now to their visions, dreams and aspirations. I confess Jeremiah 29:11 over their lives that there is a plan that has been spoken over their lives and you oh Lord has ordained an end of expectation. I prophesy a Judah anointing upon every vision and purpose that has been given unto them. They are free to worship, free to build, free to create and free to reproduce seeds according to your kind. Their wombs are open, there will be no aborted visions, miscarried or still born purposes! I speak life into their being, I speak encouragement to the now! I thank you for their assignment in this earth to show forth your praise and glory. In Jesus Mighty name I pray, Amen.

Made in the USA
Columbia, SC
20 June 2023